# A
# BOOK of NONSENSE

A

# BOOK OF NONSENSE.

## BY EDWARD LEAR.

There was an Old Derry down Derry, who loved to see little folks merry;
So he made them a Book, and with laughter they shook
At the fun of that Derry down Derry.

## The Metropolitan Museum of Art

AND

## A Studio Book · The Viking Press

NEW YORK

Published in 1980 by The Metropolitan Museum of Art
A Studio Book/The Viking Press

LIBRARY OF CONGRESS CATALOGING IN PUBLICATION DATA

Lear, Edward, 1812-1888.
  A book of nonsense.

  (A studio book)
  Reprint of the 187-? ed. published by F. Warne,
London, Scribner, Welford, New York; with new
introd.
  1. Nonsense-verses, English I. Title.

PR4879.L2N4 1980          821'.8          80-5355
ISBN 0-87099-241-4 (MMA)
ISBN 0-670-18011-4 (Viking)

Printed in Japan

# Introduction

Edward Lear, an accomplished ornithological draftsman, wrote and illustrated several journals during his European travels, and for a while acted as Queen Victoria's drawing master at Osborne House. But his real fame and fortune came from *A Book of Nonsense*, published by the London firm Thomas McLean in 1846 when he was a young man of thirty-four. Lear lived to see thirty more editions printed before he died in 1888. The book was enlarged with additional limericks and illustrations in 1861, and around 1870 a rare edition appeared with all 113 illustrations in color.

The idea for the book was born in 1832 when the Earl of Derby invited Lear to stay with him at Knowsley Hall, near Liverpool, to make drawings of the animals in his fabulous menagerie. At that time the Earl was surrounded by grandchildren, and to amuse these young companions Lear would recite verses from *Anecdotes and Adventures of Fifteen Gentlemen*, a book he had only just become acquainted with although it was published some ten years earlier. His favorite limerick began: "There was a sick man of Tobago . . ." This became the springboard for inventions of his own. The more verses Lear made up for the children, the more they chuckled and begged him to go on thinking up new ones. He then started to illustrate the limericks, basing his drawings on the scribbles he had dashed off earlier for the children, and it was inevitable that one day the best of these fanciful verses would find their way into a book.

In the first edition of *A Book of Nonsense* Lear was identified as "Derry down Derry—who loved to see little folks merry." The public did not know who the author was until his name appeared on the title page of the 1861 enlarged edition. Even then, some had their doubts. There is a story that Lear loved to tell of a train ride he took one day from London to Guildford. Two small boys, accompanied by two ladies, entered his carriage. One boy carried a copy of the 1861 edition of *A Book of Nonsense*. After seating themselves and opening the book, the boys soon started to shake with laughter. Their merriment prompted an old gentleman in the carriage to remark, "How grateful all children and parents ought to be to the statesman who has given his time composing that charming book!" The two ladies were puzzled. Then one of them took the book from the boys and showed him the title page, on which "Edward Lear" was clearly printed. The old man laughingly maintained that it was the Earl of Derby having his own little joke. "As you can see," said he, "the name LEAR is simply EARL transposed." Unable to keep silent any longer, Lear, proving his identity by displaying a hat, handkerchief, and walking stick all marked with his name and producing several letters addressed to him, managed, with great good humor, to persuade his "would-be extinguisher" that there was an artist named Lear, that *he* was that artist, and that *A Book of Nonsense* indeed was *his* book.

The most famous of Lear's other works are *Nonsense Songs, Stories, Botany and Alphabets* (1871), which includes "The Owl and the Pussy-Cat" and "The Jumblies," *More Nonsense, Pictures, Rhymes, Botany, Etc.* (1872), and *Laughable Lyrics* (1877). But apart from "The Owl and the Pussy-Cat," it is for all the wonderful limericks, such as *There was an Old Man who said, "Hush! I perceive a young bird in this bush!"* and *There was a Young Lady of Bute, who played on a silver-gilt flute* and *There was an Old Man on whose nose most birds of the air could repose*, that Edward Lear will ever be loved, imitated, and thanked the world over, by adults as well as by children.

BRYAN HOLME

Edward Lear proving his identity.
Illustration by Edward Lear
from *More Nonsense*, 1894

There was an Old Man with a beard, who said, "It is just as I feared!—
Two Owls and a Hen, four Larks and a Wren,
Have all built their nests in my beard!"

There was a Young Lady whose eyes were unique as to colour and size;
When she opened them wide, people all turned aside,
And started away in surprise.

There was a Young Girl of Majorca, whose Aunt was a very fast walker;
She walked seventy miles, and leaped fifteen stiles,
Which astonished that Girl of Majorca.

There was an Old Man with a poker, who painted his face with red ochre.
When they said, " You're a Guy! " he made no reply,
But knocked them all down with his poker.

There was a Young Lady of Russia, who screamed so that no one could hush her;
Her screams were extreme,—no one heard such a scream
As was screamed by that Lady of Russia.

There was an Old Person of Troy, whose drink was warm brandy and soy,
Which he took with a spoon, by the light of the moon,
In sight of the city of Troy.

There was a Young Lady of Clare, who was madly pursued by a Bear;
When she found she was tired, she abruptly expired,
That unfortunate Lady of Clare.

There was an Old Man in a pew, whose waistcoat was spotted with blue;
But he tore it in pieces, to give to his Nieces,
That cheerful Old Man in a pew.

There **was** an Old Person of Cadiz, who was always polite to all ladies;
But in handing his daughter, he fell into the water,
Which drowned that Old Person of Cadiz.

There was an Old Man of Peru, who watched his wife making a stew;
But once, by mistake, in a stove she did bake
That unfortunate Man of Peru.

There was an Old Man of Nepaul, from his horse had a terrible fall;
But, though split quite in two, with some very strong glue
They mended that man of Nepaul.

There was an Old Man of Marseilles, whose daughters wore bottle-green veils;
They caught several Fish, which they put in a dish,
And sent to their Pa at Marseilles.

There was an Old Man of Peru, who never knew what he should do;
So he tore off his hair, and behaved like a bear,
That intrinsic Old Man of Peru.

There was an Old Man of the West, who never could get any rest
So they set him to spin on his nose and his chin,
Which cured that Old Man of the West.

There was an Old Man of Columbia, who was thirsty, and called out for some beer;
But they brought it quite hot, in a small copper pot,
Which disgusted that man of Columbia.

There was an Old Man in a tree, who was horribly bored by a Bee;
When they said, "Does it buzz?" he replied, "Yes, it does!
It's a regular brute of a Bee!"

There was an Old Man with a gong, who bumped at it all the day long;
But they called out, "Oh law! you 're a horrid old bore!"
So they smashed that Old Man with a gong.

There was an Old Man of the Wrekin, whose shoes made a horrible creaking;
But they said, "Tell us whether your shoes are of leather,
Or of what, you Old Man of the Wrekin?"

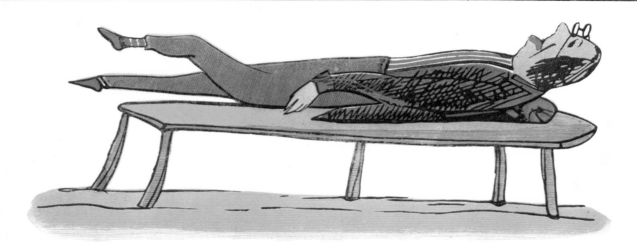

There was an Old Man of Moldavia, who had the most curious behaviour;
For while he was able, he slept on a table,
That funny Old Man of Moldavia.

There was an Old Person of Chili, whose conduct was painful and silly;
He sate on the stairs, eating apples and pears,
That imprudent Old Person of Chili.

There was an Old Lady of Chertsey, who made a remarkable curtsey;
She twirled round and round, till she sank underground,
Which distressed all the people of Chertsey.

There was an Old Person of Ischia, whose conduct grew friskier and friskier;
He danced hornpipes and jigs, and ate thousands of figs,
That lively Old Person of Ischia.

There was an Old Man of Vesuvius, who studied the works of Vitruvius;
When the flames burnt his book, to drinking he took,
That morbid Old Man of Vesuvius.

There was an Old Man of Bohemia, whose daughter was christened Euphemia;
But one day, to his grief, she married a thief,
Which grieved that Old Man of Bohemia.

There was an Old Man of Corfu, who never knew what he should do;
So he rushed up and down, till the sun made him brown,
That bewildered Old Man of Corfu.

There was an Old Lady whose folly induced
  her to sit in a holly,
Whereon, by a thorn, her dress being torn,
  She quickly became melancholy.

There was a Young Lady of Poole, whose soup was
  excessively cool;
So she put it to boil by the aid of some oil,
  That ingenious Young Lady of Poole.

There was an Old Man of Cape Horn, who wished he had never been born;
So he sat on a chair till he died of despair,
That dolorous Man of Cape Horn.

There was an Old Person of Rheims, who was troubled with horrible dreams;
So to keep him awake they fed him with cake,
Which amused that Old Person of Rheims.

There was an Old Person of Leeds, whose head was infested with beads;
She sat on a stool, and ate gooseberry-fool,
Which agreed with that person of Leeds.

There was a Young Person of Smyrna, whose Grandmother threatened to burn her;
But she seized on the Cat, and said, "Granny, burn that!
You incongruous Old Woman of Smyrna!"

There was an Old Man of the South, who had an immoderate mouth;
But in swallowing a dish that was quite full of Fish,
He was choked, that Old Man of the South.

There was an Old Man with a flute,—a " sarpint " ran into his boot!
But he played day and night, till the " sarpint " tock flight,
And avoided that man with a flute.

There was a Young Person of Crete, whose toilette was far from complete;
She dressed in a sack, spickle-speckled with black,
That ombliferous person of Crete.

There was a Young Lady of Norway, who casually sat in a doorway;
When the door squeezed her flat, she exclaimed, "What of that?"
This courageous Young Lady of Norway.

There was an Old Person of Rhodes, who strongly objected to toads;
He paid several cousins to catch them by dozens,
That futile Old Person of Rhodes.

There was a Young Lady of Bute, who played on a silver-gilt flute;
She played several jigs to her Uncle's white Pigs:
That amusing Young Lady of Bute.

There was an Old Man in a casement, who held up his hands in amazement;
When they said, "Sir, you'll fall!" he replied, "Not at all!"
That incipient Old Man in a casement.

There was a Young Lady of Dorking, who bought a large bonnet for walking;
But its colour and size so bedazzled her eyes,
That she very soon went back to Dorking.

There was an Old Person of Prague, who was suddenly seized with the plague;
But they gave him some butter, which caused him to mutter,
And cured that Old Person of Prague.

There was a Young Lady of Portugal, whose ideas were excessively nautical;
She climbed up a tree to examine the sea,
But declared she would never leave Portugal.

There was an Old Person whose habits induced him to feed upon Rabbits;
When he'd eaten eighteen, he turned perfectly green,
Upon which he relinquished those habits.

There was an Old Man of Berlin, whose form was uncommonly thin ;
 Till he once, by mistake, was mixed up in a cake,
  So they baked that Old Man of Berlin.

There was a Young Lady of Parma, whose conduct grew calmer and calmer ;
When they said "Are you dumb?" she merely said "Hum !"
That provoking Young Lady of Parma.

There was an Old Person of Philœ, whose conduct was scroobious and wily ;
 He rushed up a Palm when the weather was calm,
  And observed all the ruins of Philœ.

There was an Old Person of Spain, who hated all trouble and pain;
So he sate on a chair with his feet in the air,
That umbrageous Old Person of Spain.

There was an Old Person of Dover, who rushed through a field of blue clover;
But some very large Bees stung his nose and his knees,
So he very soon went back to Dover.

There was an Old Person of Dutton, whose head was as small as a button ;
So to make it look big, he purchased a wig,
And rapidly rushed about Dutton.

There was an Old Man who supposed that the street door was partially closed ;
But some very large Rats ate his coats and his hats,
While that futile Old Gentleman dozed.

There was a Young Lady whose chin resembled the point of a pin ;
So she had it made sharp, and purchased a harp,
And played several tunes with her chin.

There was a Young Lady whose bonnet came untied when the birds sate upon it ;
But she said, " I don't care ! all the birds in the air
Are welcome to sit on my bonnet ! "

There was a Young Lady of Ryde, whose shoe-strings were seldom untied;
She purchased some clogs, and some small spotty Dogs,
And frequently walked about Ryde.

There was an Old Person of Gretna, who rushed down the crater of Etna;
When they said, "Is it hot?" he replied, "No, it's not!"
That mendacious Old Person of Gretna.

There was an Old Person of Hurst, who drank when he was not athirst;
When they said, "You'll grow fatter!" he answered, "What matter?"
That globular Person of Hurst.

There was an Old Man on a hill, who seldom, if ever, stood still;
He ran up and down in his Grandmother's gown,
Which adorned that Old Man on a hill.

There was an Old Man of the West, who wore a pale plum-coloured vest;
When they said, "Does it fit?" he replied, "Not a bit!"
That uneasy Old Man of the West.

There was an Old Person of Buda, whose conduct grew ruder and ruder.
Till at last with a hammer they silenced his clamour,
By smashing that Person of Buda.

There was an Old Man of the Isles, whose face was pervaded with smiles;
He sang "High dum diddle," and played on the fiddle,
That amiable Man of the Isles.

There was an Old Man of Kilkenny, who never had more than a penny;
He spent all that money in onions and honey,
That wayward Old Man of Kilkenny.

There was a Young Lady whose nose was so long that it reached to her toes;
So she hired an Old Lady, whose conduct was steady,
To carry that wonderful nose.

There was an Old Man with a nose, who said, "If you choose to suppose
That my nose is too long, you are certainly wrong!"
That remarkable Man with a nose.

There was an Old Man of the Hague, whose ideas were excessively vague;
He built a balloon to examine the moon,
That deluded Old Man of the Hague.

There was an Old Man who said, "Hush! I perceive a young bird in this bush!"
When they said, "Is it small?" he replied, "Not at all!
It is four times as big as the bush!"

There was an Old Man of the Nile, who sharpened his nails with a file,
Till he cut off his thumbs, and said calmly, " This comes
Of sharpening one's nails with a file ! "

There was an Old Man of Whitehaven, who danced a quadrille with a Raven;
But they said, " It's absurd to encourage this bird ! "
So they smashed that Old Man of Whitehaven.

There was an Old Man of Coblenz, the length of whose legs was immense;
He went with one prance from Turkey to France,
That surprising Old Man of Coblenz.

There was an Old Man on some rocks, who shut his Wife up in a box:
When she said, "Let me out," he exclaimed, "Without doubt
You will pass all your life in that box."

There was an Old Man of the Dee, who was sadly annoyed by a Flea:
When he said, " I will scratch it ! " they gave him a hatchet,
Which grieved that Old Man of the Dee.

There was an Old Man of Calcutta, who perpetually ate bread and butter;
Till a great bit of muffin, on which he was stuffing,
Choked that horrid Old Man of Calcutta.

There was an Old Person of Cromer, who stood on one leg to read Homer;
When he found he grew stiff, he jumped over the cliff,
Which concluded that Person of Cromer.

There was a Young Lady of Hull, who was chased by a virulent Bull;
But she seized on a spade, and called out, "Who's afraid!"
Which distracted that virulent Bull.

There was an Old Man of Aôsta, who possessed a large Cow, but he lost her;
But they said, "Don't you see she has rushed up a tree?
You invidious Old Man of Aôsta!"

There was a Young Lady of Sweden, who went by the slow train to Weedon;
When they cried, "Weedon Station!" she made no observation,
But thought she should go back to Sweden.

There was a Young Lady of Troy, whom several large Flies did annoy;
Some she killed with a thump, some she drowned at the pump,
And some she took with her to Troy.

There was an Old Man who said, "How shall I flee from this horrible Cow?
I will sit on this stile, and continue to smile,
Which may soften the heart of that Cow."

There was an Old Man on whose nose most birds of the air could repose;
But they all flew away at the closing of day,
Which relieved that Old Man and his nose.

There was an Old Person of Sparta, who had twenty-five sons and one "darter;"
He fed them on Snails, and weighed them in scales,
That wonderful Person of Sparta.

There was an Old Man with an Owl, who continued to bother and howl;
He sat on a rail, and imbibed bitter ale,
Which refreshed that Old Man and his Owl.

There was an Old Person of Ems, who casually fell in the Thames;
And when he was found, they said he was drowned,
That unlucky Old Person of Ems.

There was an Old Man of Dundee, who frequented the top of a tree;
When disturbed by the Crows, he abruptly arose,
And exclaimed, "I'll return to Dundee!"

There was an Old Man who said, "Well! will
*nobody* answer this bell?
I have pulled day and night, till my hair has
grown white,
But nobody answers this bell!"

There was an Old Person of Ewell, who chiefly
subsisted on gruel;
But to make it more nice, he inserted some
Mice,
Which refreshed that Old Person of Ewell.

There was a Young Lady of Welling, whose praise all the world was a-telling;
She played on the harp, and caught several Carp,
That accomplished Young Lady of Welling.

There was an Old Person of Cheadle was put in the stocks by the Beadle
For stealing some pigs, some coats, and some wigs,
That horrible Person of Cheadle.

There was an Old Man of Madras, who rode on a cream-coloured Ass;
But the length of its ears so promoted his fears,
That it killed that Old Man of Madras.

There was an Old Man in a boat, who said, "I'm afloat! I'm afloat!"
When they said, "No, you ain't!" he was ready to faint,
That unhappy Old Man in a boat.

There was an Old Man of the North, who fell into a basin of broth;
But a laudable Cook fished him out with a hook,
Which saved, that Old Man of the North.

There was an Old Man of Apulia, whose conduct was very peculiar;
He fed twenty sons upon nothing but buns,
That whimsical Man of Apulia.

There was a Young Lady of Turkey, who wept
    when the weather was murky;
When the day turned out fine, she ceased to
    repine,
        That capricious Young Lady of Turkey.

There was an Old Man of Quebec,—a beetle ran
    over his neck;
But he cried, "With a needle I'll slay you, O
    beadle!"
        That angry Old Man of Quebec.

There was an Old Person of Mold, who shrank from sensations of cold;
So he purchased some muffs, some furs, and some fluffs,
    And wrapped himself well from the cold.

There was an Old Man of Vienna, who lived upon Tincture of Senna;
When that did not agree, he took Camomile Tea,
That nasty Old Man of Vienna.

There was an Old Person of Basing, whose presence of mind was amazing;
He purchased a steed, which he rode at full speed,
And escaped from the people of Basing.

There was an Old Man of th' Abruzzi, so blind that he couldn't his foot see;
When they said, "That's your toe," he replied, "Is it so?"
That doubtful Old Man of th' Abruzzi.

There was an Old Man of the East, who gave all his children a feast;
But they all ate so much, and their conduct was such,
That it killed that Old Man of the East.

There was an Old Man of Melrose, who walked on the tips of his toes;
But they said, "It ain't pleasant to see you at present,
You stupid Old Man of Melrose."

There was a Young Lady of Lucca, whose lovers completely forsook her;
She ran up a tree, and said "Fiddle-de-dee!"
Which embarrassed the people of Lucca.

There was a Young Lady of Wales, who caught a large Fish without scales;
When she lifted her hook, she exclaimed, "Only look!"
    That ecstatic Young Lady of Wales.

There was an Old Person of Burton, whose answers were rather uncertain;
When they said, "How d'ye do?" he replied, "Who are you?"
    That distressing Old Person of Burton.

There was an Old Man of the coast, who placidly sat on a post;
But when it was cold he relinquished his hold,
And called for some hot buttered toast.

There was an Old Lady of Prague, whose language was horribly vague;
When they said, "Are these caps?" she answered, "Perhaps!"
That oracular Lady of Prague.

There was an Old Man with a beard, who sat on a Horse when he reared;
But they said, "Never mind! you will fall off behind,
You propitious Old Man with a beard!"

There was an Old Person of Tring, who embellished his nose with a ring;
He gazed at the moon every evening in June,
That ecstatic Old Person of Tring.

There was an Old Man of Kamschatka, who possessed a remarkably fat Cur;
His gait and his waddle were held as a model
To all the fat dogs in Kamschatka.

There was an Old Man of Leghorn, the smallest that ever was born;
But quickly snapt up he was once by a Puppy,
Who devoured that Old Man of Leghorn.

There was an Old Person of Tartary, who divided his jugular artery;
But he screeched to his Wife, and she said, "Oh, my life!
Your death will befelt by all Tartary!"

There was an Old Person of Chester, whom several small children did pester;
They threw some large stones, which broke most of his bones,
And displeased that Old Person of Chester.

There was an Old Person of Anerley, whose conduct was strange and unmannerly;
He rushed down the Strand with a Pig in each hand,
But returned in the evening to Anerley.

There was a Young Lady of Tyre, who swept the loud chords of a lyre;
At the sound of each sweep she enraptured the deep,
And enchanted the city of Tyre.

There was an Old Man of the Cape, who possessed a large Barbary Ape;
Till the Ape, one dark night, set the house all alight,
Which burned that Old Man of the Cape.

There was an Old Person of Bangor, whose face was distorted with anger;
He tore off his boots, and subsisted on roots,
That borascible Person of Bangor.